Pieces of You and Me

By
Tina Nicole Williams

Published by True Beginnings Publishing.
Copyright 2016.

ISBN-13: 978-0692683422
ISBN-10: 0692683429

Ordering Information:
To order additional copies of this book, please visit Amazon or CreateSpace, at: https://www.createspace.com/6180120

Pieces of You and Me
© Tina Nicole Williams.
First Printing, 2016

True Beginnings Publishing

Dedication

Poetry is much more than an art form with lines, meters, metaphors and rhythm. If it does not resonate or move the heart and mind of the reader, the beauty of it is lost. My heart and soul are devoted to the words within this book. Encased in every poem is all that has come to consume me, for love is fierce and extraordinary.

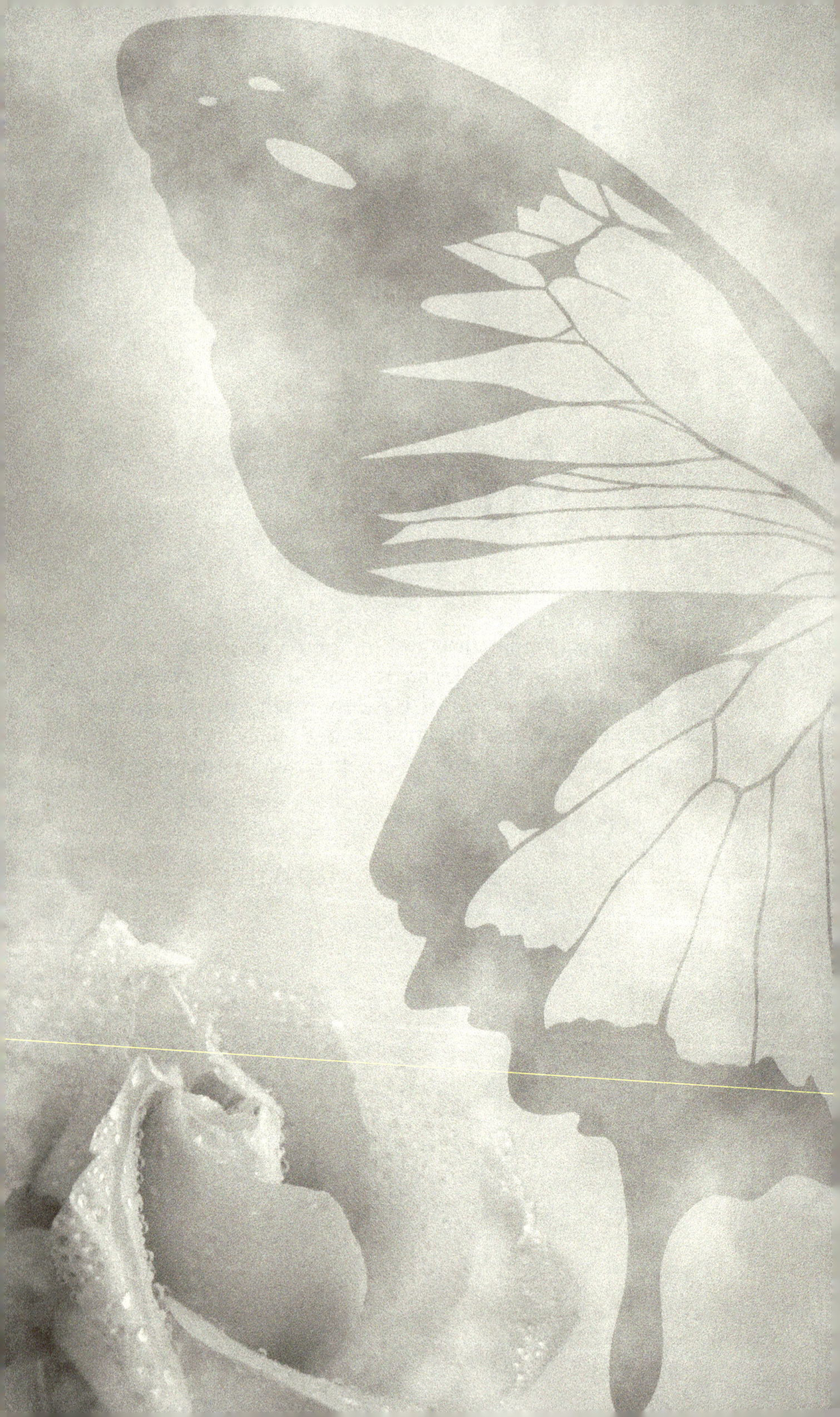

"There's only you and I in the wake of this moment…
Only you and I to bear the blame if we sully the shine of it.
For love and love alone has led us to this juncture…
Will we journey on as one or part at this fork in the road
And remain un-remembered?"

Table of Contents

Love and I

Seasons Change

The Birth of Passion

Love and I

Love and I

Love and I sat as friends...
in the chill of a November day...
We spoke of the freshness of the morning wind...
The spilled radiance of the sun in a peppered, gray sky...
We spoke of moonlight and stardust...
Things that make us laugh...
things that make us cry...
And at the height of the crisper noonday...
We spoke of romance and passion...
Touches and whispers...
in a lover's bed...
I became both hearer and ear...
blessed by the words...
Love and I sat as friends...
in the chill of a November day...
And my heart reached toward love...
As I took my pen and wrote my love on paper.

Storm Chaser

You came into me like the quickening in a storm...
Come again to me that way.
When I am with you...
my soul finds its joy,
And without you...
love vanishes into the clouds.
Today, the sky whispers...
you are near...
Come again to me that way...

Inside

Love sits beside me...
cherished and comfortable...
especially on dark days when thoughts
are blurry and clarity cannot be seen.

On these days...

Love walks hand in hand with me
down winding paths where nothing else exists
but love and I... in the quiet of the day.
Love then turned to me and said...
"Listen to your soul speak...
Looking outside of yourself
soils your heart, your thoughts...
and leaves you empty."

In the Knowing

Love and I... face to face at last...
remembering the dark of our fall...
recalling the presence of our winter...
when the threads of my pulse ran cold.

Do you remember, love,
when the fire turned to ashes...
and we sought the forever spring in us...
for we feared this space between life and death
without the encounter of human touch...

Come to me, love, like a jealous river...
Eager to be a part of a frenzied sea.
Love finds comfort in knowing
You and I will always be.

Thoughts of You

Love, I have never stopped looking for you...
never became disenchanted with your allure.
For in dreams, I have seen your lucid eyes...
just before dawn... when your soul spoke to me.
Today I found you in the rain... and I cried...
and your lips eagerly sought the taste of my tears.

I wish you could see me sheathed in my eagerness...
for I am student of your bewitching passion...
possessed by the impressions of you
that leaves me forever consumed.
I have spent a lifetime it seems...
marinating in these thoughts of you...

Love, lead me to a sky that's wide enough
that I may bask beneath your shine...
for one brief moment in your presence...
No matter where... until then, love...
I will look for signs that you are within reach...

The Moment and You

Slow... he walked into the well of my darkness...
Paused... for an intimate moment
as he viewed the perverse walls of my guilt and pain.
I imprisoned my heart, hid my emotions,
and placed blood-tinged vows in shadow boxes,
never to endure the bereft tears of love again.
Quietly... I stood on the sidelines of my isolation...
curious to trace the roots of his fascination...
all the while breathless
as his conversation danced and sang...
hushing my sobbing ears.
He held a timeless pen within hand
as he searched through my timeless truths...
promising to rekindle the flame of my silent hunger
with a muse... wrapped in to have and to hold...
armed with fire and desire to rupture time...
space... and return my captive heart...
the dowry of this verse... his to love
and moments like this to be remembered.

When Love Comes

Like a cool morning rain
falling from an August sky...
love pierced the old of me...
unveiling my sweetness...
Love kissed my tears...
swallowed the sting of my pain.
And like a melody that comes to mind to stay,
Love reopened unremembered emotions...
The bread...
wine...
fruit of love that makes the heart listen.

From my head...
to the shine in my eyes,
to the tips of my feet,
Love found me beautiful...
despite the tracks of nettled scars...
For Love took me within the swerve of its arms...
bringing all senses close...
in touch with my skin.
Now nothing is closed off or forgotten...
the taste of my mouth...
the warmth of my skin knows these things...
I have lost nothing.

A Love Poem

Beloved, turn off the lights... speak to me...
Is your heart to be evermore my own?
Does my name slip from your lips... silently...
Content... that I should need ne'er more to moan.

Beloved... watch close love's acquainted eyes...
Reflections hold no secrets from within.
For the soul's bidding eyes will ne'er tell lies.
Remember... doubt not... your want is my sin.

Beloved... wilt thou walk with me through dreams...
Come lay with me as if I were dying...
Kiss my mouth... give me water from your stream...
Listen, love... the voice of the rain is crying.

Love lives through winter's cold... summer's fire...
Though daylight begins... and night retires.

Possession

He stood too far left...
to sense the sway in my glances...
Head turned downwind...
to the voodoo of my fragrant sap.
Alas, disarmed by his charms,
I would dare stay the course;
unleashed... yet bound to possess
the familiar in his eyes.

The cadence of my steps silenced the ground...
and just like a silhouette drapes over the moon,
I brushed past the dawn of a storm
to solicit the zephyr's breath;
to tender my wants...
through ardent whispers in his ear.

And on that faithful night... oh,
how my heart thrums in celebration...
reviving love.
Now the tourniquet once applied to passion
has no power and must loose its hold.

You, a stranger before me...
a dream sought... conjured real.
Nostalgic, I'll undress these filthy scars of vulnerability
to stand naked before you... unencumbered...
by masks and fraudulent roles that one can possess.

He is my sanctuary... where my walls fall down.
I would betray all else... for he feeds my soul.
To exist within his space and time... intoxicates...
I cannot peel myself away from his sleight of hand.
Addictive, I have become... seeker of his warmth.

Tonight, the earth shook
and the moon called out his name...
as he turned... moving right through me.

She Is

She is his whisper...
the catalyst of his thoughts...
the ache that stirs his needs...
the conductor of his heart.

She is his eyes...
the perfect vision in his sight...
a constant in all his daydreams...
arousing his dreams at night.

She is his touch...
that heightens what he feels...
the stroke that fuels his passion...
the fruition of every spill.

Spellbound

I will love you until love becomes immortal,
until this chaotic world with its caustic tears
dries up like dust... loses its convicted trace
to morning smiles and my hand in yours,
to Oceanside walks while the blue sky dances,
to late night pillow talk and moonlight glances.

I will love you until love becomes immortal,
until those cracked and wrecked memories
that provoke your fears and pains
are buried alive, left for dead
and nothing's left
but a soft caress of my silhouette.

I will love you until love becomes immortal,
until songs can be heard in the sound of silence
in the vast air, aboveground
and in the secrets that lie beneath.

I will love you until love becomes immortal...
I live only for the want of your smile;
for with you, my heart
has found its home in this life...
and in death, I will only love you still.
I surrender this truth just for a taste of your lips
that has me Spellbound...

Lost in Love

Through keyed-up days, unspent nights,
I walked unruly ruts in washed-out roads... left to right,
desirous to encounter a glimpse of love's silhouette.
Yet, I've only inhaled its aura amongst the breeze.
I have travelled rough paths of cunning despair
beneath the ruptured sky and the sun's pale halo.
I have fended off love's demise from the dread of doubts,
summoned by the frantic feel of the calescent rain.

Love... I hunger for it more than food;
this breath of life that sustains me...
finds no other source to sate its yearning;
left parched... I am thirsty for its quench.

I crave to look in love's eyes... become its reflection;
douse my soul within its silken flesh.
I crave love's mouth and love-drenched kisses;
love's tender voice... pillow talk whispers.

I have felt love near my garden's gate,
mere shadows length away.
I long to kneel at love's feet...
tend to its wants and draw it to myself.
I have waited a lifetime it seems,
hoping it would enter in.

Life is but a little while,
and love is its greatest treasure.
My heart is full of old battle scars,
and the patches I used
to piece it together again...
I've kept,
for it strengthens the love that I offer.

Love, do not turn from me...
for I am lost without your presence...
and this want claims my days and nights.
Come, love, peer through the haze
and hidden doors... where my heart lays scattered

For Love

For love, have you ever wandered down a road
foreign to your footsteps, dismissing anxieties and fears,
without knowing if you will ever return home again?
Have you ever defied a storm as it raged upon your path,
dared the breath of the wind to sway you from its course,
or scoffed at the rain to touch your soul?

For love, have you ever gave another your all,
only to walk away empty, raped of tears,
or lay drowning, consumed with pain...
but your heart beat on because love still lived?
Have you ever danced when you could not walk,
lain beneath the shine of a harvest moon,
bathing in the purity of its light
while listening for your beating heart,
only to hear the cries of the world inside?

And for love, have you ever torn down your walls,
exposing the you that is said to be wonderfully made,
prancing around with all your frailties, weakness and shame?
Have you ever committed yourself to something, someone,
other than yourself, or gave your all for what you believed in?
Could you, would you... for love?

Love; The Vein of Poetry

You are my poetry; indigo blue, sandalwood-scented ink...
Wordsmith of my heart; sole author of my earthly wants.
You are the physical embodiment of all that engages my senses.
In lucid daydreams, thoughts of you gather as lyrical phrases...
serenading the space above and beneath
the source of my life's essence.

You are my poetry; subtle hues of passion...
words that seduce and woo me...
the forever verses... where only you and I exist;
A legacy of romance encased in twin flame metaphors.
In a leather-bound book of parchment paper,
words and more words come spilling,
clinging to each other as I pen...
I love you... backward and forward...
In a language only you and I can understand.

You are my poetry; the impetus that brands my fevered flesh,
forging words that move right through me.
How I savour the taste of you on my lips,
the familiar of your touch...
so unrelenting in their seduction;
but in poetry, you and I are unleashed
as adjectives, nouns and verbs...
So much so that the moon knows us personally.

You are my poetry; the Nairobi gold of a blazing noon sun;
the fascination of a new day that surrenders
to black velvet curtains drawn round me at night.
You are my poetry, the fevered forbidden dance
etched to grace the page of passionate prose.

You are my poetry... the inhales and exhales...
that leaves me shuddering;
and like an orgasm emanating from an un-robed muse,
you guide my hips to bask beneath your afterglow
when words alone are impotent and silent.

What Pearl Are You?

I am in the midst of the seasons,
solstice and equinox.
The house of my spirit is blessed,
smooth as the rivers run,
firm as the miraculous mountains
where the sun descends to rest.
I am a sojourner in this life...
existing in breath and pulse.

I am as subtle as a southern breeze,
fervent as the outcry of the pounding rain.
My heart is fated, having known pure ecstasy
before it was seduced by words.
It was written in a tender letter
on the cusp of my soul;
if you desire to read it,
become a seeker of my heart,
a companion to my soul;
there's no need to spill it here.

I'm both companion and confessor,
both lover and welcomed guest.
Yet, dampness has strolled down my face...
leaking traces of yours and my encounter.

I am the muse to the poet's pen,
that spontaneous Zen of creative thought;
speaker of my house till journey's end.
You knock and ask "What pearl are you?"
I'll smile... humbly reply; "I am love."

Silently Musing

Breathe lightly; listen from left to right
armed with discernment.
Become as one, from front to back.
Free your loving and your heart
to rest in the midst of the present.
Pray that the moon and sun rises...
sets each day, with gratitude and reverence,
for we own no second of it or its glory.
Learn to dance with the feet of another,
sing from your soul without beats or lyrics;
let the words flow like harps and bells
that swirls the leaves.
Befriend the mirror,
for sight is distorted by mere eyes alone;
the ego is easily fooled by words... looks... actions.
Become foolishly in love, without course or expectations.
Shout it into the wind,
then give it voice within the beauty of a poem.
Empty yourself inside until there's nothing left
but the spirit's serenity and the presence of God.

So Close

Midst the dark of night,
beneath the veil of moonlight,
I wait for you
though my eyes have never lost sight of your face,
always in touch with your hand.
Somewhere in time
is where we'll begin,
Consummating our moment,
for an eternity to share.

Until then,
make love to me with words,
echo them within my mind and heart...
that my soul may dwell in love.

Through many flames
our love has endured.
We have sewn our seeds
beyond the depths of ordinary,
drowning out hate
and reaping love's serenity.

So tonight, I will dream you here,
so close to see the love in your eyes
and drown inside the pool of your need;
so close that we breathe as one.

Camelot

Oh how sweet were the dreams of yesterday,
fleeting moments in time now gone astray.
The days were ours to own when we first met,
time etched in memory I'll ne'er forget.
When I gave my heart to you, I feared not,
the love I found with you in Camelot.

Oh how sweet were the dreams of yesterday,
longing for night to come and steal the day,
that I may close my eyes to welcome sleep,
where in slumber's hushed pose your presence creeps;
to consummate our love that none dare stop,
the love I found with you in Camelot.

Oh how sweet were the dreams of yesterday,
embraced in your arms, I so long to stay.
To share with you all that life has to give,
vowing my love for as long as I live;
for eternity ne'er to be forgot,
the love I found with you in Camelot.

Ruled by Love

Love's exposed my vulnerabilities,
praised me as it dressed me in poetry,
exchanged emptiness for a beautiful existence;
eyes and mind cracked,
open with clarity of thought.

Love's unchained restraints,
freeing my voice that was stuck on mute;
no longer chaste or polite,
quick to laugh and sing.

Love's released echoes
from the confines of my chest,
swept the doorway of my heart,
preparing for its special guest.
And today I can laugh
at what scorned me yesterday;
free of who I was,
embraced within the shine.
Come
observe me in my quietness,
for I am...
yet I am not,
a lit hearth, burning water,
a ripening seeker,
full of heart and soul;
an Alchemist of Love.

Enchanted

Never have I seen the moon so bright before.
Its shine glows with radiance that would shame the sun;

Yet... it falls short of a perfect splendour,
when in the presence of you.

For, my love, your eyes reflect the brilliance of the stars
that I wish upon each night.

You are the possessor of my conscious hopes,
keeper of my seen and unseen dreams.

Nothing else moves me or makes love to my soul

Intoxication

I am drunk on the fragrance of your essence.
The scent of it stirred the breath of a luring breeze,
arousing the spirit of my slumbering love.
And I searched for you with hungry eyes
of a heart held prisoner by the desire of its own longings.

I found you;
on a night when the sky was lit by shooting stars.
You were shadow aligned with the moon...
consumed by a fire... rekindled in love poems.
Soft, I ran my hand down your delirious impression;
now I am infected.

I seeped through your veins
and flowed as life through your blood.
I danced within the yearning of your flesh;
found shelter in the comfort of your bones...
until you reached for me with outstretched arms,
and the love once birthed beneath a midnight sun
erased the seasons... and I fell as tears from your eyes.

Face to face... disarmed and naked,
dusty minds melted into memory...
soaring past the mortal confines of our body.
Tonight, we'll rewrite the repeat of our history.
For our love has endured in and out many lifetimes;
I simply lost my way... now I am home.
Come, love... for time grows short... my soul is spent;
let our hearts fall into one rhythm.

You are here, secured within the well of my soul;
never to breathe again without you.
For I have opened the door to love's house
and made room for you to reside in it,
peeling away all that's come before this moment.

Now, speak sweet things into my ears,
brush upon my famished needs
and lay me down upon a bed with sheets of passion.
I can no longer tell where you begin and I end...
for we are one; I am Intoxicated.

Speak Words to Me

Speak words of love to me,
let them spill like a ceaseless flood
filling the places within my chest,
once-hidden from the sting of pain.

Speak words of love to me
when the sun bids adieu to day
and evening's prism rainbow
lends to the still of the moment.

Free your voice with sweetness
like the night bird's song,
imbued with poetry
that feeds and soothes the soul.

Carry me up past the dark roll of clouds
wrapped within the sweat of your eagerness.

With You

In your eyes,
I am beautiful.
By your arms,
I am warmed,
and in your heart I am at home,
falling in love with you.

Timeless Love

Touched by your impression, moments became timeless
and the merciless silence of the moon and stars
succumbed to intimate laurels... boasting fevered refrains.
If not for the genuineness in the ooze of your voice,
I'd accuse you of sorcery, for you drew me in like no other.

Imprisoned words tragically kept from these lips
emerged as an unleashed thirst... triggered by your heat.
All that bled my heart slipped from memory...
I no longer tasted the bitterness of my tears;
the air was renewed with the fragrance of love... and you.

Inebriated by your warmth, I no longer looked back,
finding refuge where my heart longs to reside today.
We were destined to be in love... love;
you and I have always dwelled in a bed of memories
on a reclusive shore, parched and waiting...
for a meant day's dawning to wash ashore.

My soul is consumed by all that is of you;
I have shed my armour, allow me to soothe your pain away,
and I'll remind you every day till the sun no longer rises;
fortunate am I... I love you.

Bridges to the Soul

There is solace here,
shelter from the chaos of the world,
where silence is treasured
and talking is akin to insolence.

Let the tongue stay quiet….
Nature is gifting us with living poetry.

Hush, magnify your ears to hear,
undress your eyes from the sinful veil
of this earthly canvass;
behold the greatest artistry of life.

Surrender thought;
serenity overcomes sadness,
and the fear of death departs.

Laugh like a child at play…
for here your soul runs free.
Why are you lying here in the valley
when the bridge is just ahead?

Come, place one foot before the other...
give up this fight to be the shepherd,
become a lamb within the flock.
Trust in the source of all consciousness...

Take refuge for a while in the heart's secret place.
Listen as the songbird serenades.

Breathe the perfumed air
wafting down from the heavens.
Can you feel it... all nature is jubilant.
You are blessed... For the Beloved is here!

Our Time

It's our time; the cracks have been sealed;
infected hearts torn apart, once left scrambling in the void,
have been reassembled by deft and nimble fingers
of love under will.
Embezzled dreams held captive
by fraudulent nightmares have returned
to relish the dawn of each new tomorrow,
embraced by the convalescent sun,
envied beneath
the gaze of a green-eyed moon.

It's our time; even though we may stumble, fumble,
tracking tears that once lined our face,
now the tattler of our desires.
As we now lay less than innocent,
slow to release each frenzied surge;
my heart's found its sanctuary
inside your loving eyes.
And all is as it should be,
for it's our time.

And when all is said and done,
when greedy seas of passion dissolves soft as summer's rain...
it's our time to lay in the hush of the moment,
thankful that we survived yet another un-promised day.
For whatever the future holds
in this world that's so undone...
you are here next to me,
and it's our time;
our time to love.

In the Stillness

Enough words; I have come to ease...
heal the soul of my senses,
once laced with suede lips like rose petals,
now littered with bitter flowers,
behind veils of thorns.

I have thrown my vileness
into the mirror's heart,
escaping the prison of my ego.
Oh, how sweet
the fragrance of freedom's breath.

I have been drenched
in love's flood;
come face to face
with what was meant to be cherished.

My heart has become my head,
reclaiming master to my existence.
My soul is on fire, aroused by passion;
freed prisoner from this worldly life.
And I now dance with my eyes
and see with my ears,
finding dreams the mind has held in secret.

Enough words,
enough words;
for they tremble like leaves,
refusing to let go.
Be silent and at peace
within this moment.

Freedom

The sweet essence of you
courses through my veins,
easing the pain of my existence;
erasing the stench
of fraudulent promises and hope,
bleeding the wounds, that I may heal.
So, now, here I stand
stripped of secrets;
this moment is all that remains.
Through you,
I have found the courage to shed chains
that've bound me down;
now I'm free.

Voodoo

In your eyes, I am consumed,
in lucid shades of a wraparound rainbow...
whose colors I have yet to recognize.
In your arms, a spell unfolds about me;
and I whisper beneath my breath...
peel away this lace.

I have followed your beloved trail;
come with me or take me with you.
I have laid in the memorable
of tender moments
where I danced within your pulse,
seeped through your veins and fell
as tears to kiss the fire in your eyes...
because I love.

We are the déjà vu aromas
from another time in an endless generation
that leaves us drenched in its vigor.
Please cherish the ardor of our romance...

And when distance impedes our endless touch,
I will be as a dulcet breeze upon your burning sun,
the rhythmic ink within your pen.
When your mind yearns to soar,
I will be the dream that dreams me real.

In the midst of silver moons and crimson tides,
I hum with a voice full of hope in forevermore,
for your fingertips on the undress of my skin testifies,
you are the hope in my destiny.

My love... songs of sirens arouses the breath,
and precious time is wasting away,
so come love me today
and tomorrow we will start over again.

Seasons Change

Remember Me

Remember me... when distance impedes our touch.
Lose yourself in sweet memory's lullaby...
while the comfort of my love fills you, complete.
For I am etched upon your lamenting heart,
keeping silent company within your soul...
Always where you are.

Dread not when twilight fades to black...
spreading helter-skelter shadows on vacant walls.
For each night, I dream you here...
inside the sanctum of my arms...
Flesh of my flesh... releasing our imprisoned needs,
until dawn steals the night... yet remembered still.

Remember me even though you stagger on misery,
and the loneliness steals the ether from your mind.
Just call my name... hold me tight within your eyes,
and I will be there... never again to depart.
I will shed the veil of this fraudulent world,
to breathe you in... to bask in the hunger of your touch.

Remember me when distance impedes our touch.

Lose yourself in sweet memory's lullaby...

while the comfort of my love fills you, complete.

For I am etched upon your lamenting heart,

keeping silent company within your soul...

Always, Always, where you are.

The Breath that She Keeps

Quietly, dawn sneaks in... lifting the blinds of night;
revealing the lapis lazuli gem of heaven's eyes.
Titillating wisps of honeysuckle breezes slip through
the cracks in the window... stirring me from a death-like slumber.

The garden is wet with the sweet balm of dew,
flowers with rainbow blushes are in bloom...
the dust of yesterday washed from their vulnerable faces;
my heart once again dons its cobwebby gown of envy.

I have lost my wants; my needs are now sweat on the sheets.
Yet, something is remembered... of all the things once said,
of all the keepsake memories and intimacies we shared;
there are many flesh-drenched confessions in this old bed spring.

Beyond the quiet of the door... scents of breakfast fill the air;
aromas of fresh morning blend and banana bread.
My anxious breath arouses my pulse... and thoughts of you
once again become the focus of this frozen moment.

You pay no rent here, no closet houses your clothes,
the mail bears my name... there's no signs that one was ever two.
So tell me, how is it that you reside in my grandest of rooms...
my soul and my heart?

If We Must Part

If we must part, my love... let it be like this...
arouse me with a subtle caress...
smear my lips with scents of passion.
Intoxicate me with hunger...
come possess me once more...
and leave me... a drunken fool in love.
Do not leave me in
early morning's shrouded haze
as I lay... still enslaved
on the fringes of night's sleep.
Do not leave me disarmed...
wilting in my heart's tears...
if we must part.

If we must part,
let it be walking hand in hand
on serenity's shore...
as the moonlight dances
'cross an unruffled sea.
Say no words to me...
let our eyes to soul speak...
for mere words are impotent
where love resides.
Remember
the hush between our lips...
the sweet of our consummation...
for you are my heart's devotion.
Cherish the stillness, my love...
if we must part.

Together; Apart

I endure long days...
insufferable routines...
bleeding me... blind.
And each tic of the old clock's hand
taunts... and reminds me
of time's irreversible passing.

I must then endure the heart's control
of the highs... lows... of my senses...
when... where... my hand goes... touches,
where my foot... falls... moves in dance.
And in the mirror of eyes...
these lonesome urges...
gather momentum...
bettering sanity with untamed thoughts;
in prostration... I become a beggar
yearning for night's beloved company.

Twilight;
the swaggering zephyr whispers
into my anxiously enthused ear;
each stroke of the levitating breeze...
a reminiscing scratch and sniff...
climbing the beat of my pulse.

As night draws its curtain,
I lay bathed within its obsidian shawl,
awaiting dreamland's hocus pocus...
the realm where he invades...
where coming is past... present... future,
here at the juncture of famished desire,
and flesh's insatiable greed.

REM's siren begins to stroke
seen... unseen... triggers.
I am once again caught up... poised
beneath the cadence of his passion...
suspended by singed kisses...
doused with the thrills of this sex eddy...
breathless... as if bareback riding...
through the quivers of a March wind...
reclaiming the surge of his fevered vein
that keeps me dissolving in tireless satisfaction.

Morning comes too soon...
I am still drunk inside
night's paradigm of arousal...
it's unleashing of the coveted treasure.
And like liquid sex on the tongue,
tended... unintended...
night has become my wanton obsession.

I'm neither reckoned nor wrecked,
liberated or ashamed by this inherited dream;
together... apart...
I'm but the cradle to his ache... fuel to his fire,
the Sumerian haze that captures his eyes;
his paradise... craved... in sheer lingerie.

Cracks in a Pulseless Heart

Here, in this wrecked house,
passion is corrupted,
and there's molded love
in the cracks of the threshold...
tragic are the reticent echoes within.
The air is infected with the stench
of rotting hope... rotting dreams...
Scents suffocate and I am apt to scream...
but the silence is just too loud...
time is stressing with its second-guessing.
Yet, when I close my eyes,
these dire walls are dressed in lights,
teasing with glimpses of familiar eyes...
recalling love that held no reflection in the mirror.
I once dared to walk in love's parallel world,
and the ache in each step tore my heart...
There were times I would have laid with death
as it's shameful concubine.
Now I live each day... going in circles...
wearing this mask of nonsense...
only he and I know the truth...
beneath is broken...
waiting to be eulogized.

Sunken Footprints

Life has entrusted me with tragedies;
fractured images in my mind
that lay heavy on my spirit.
For the verve within my soul is no longer present.
It wanders without love or joy;
etching crystal lines across my heart,
stealing ether from my pulse.
Bring back the love that I have lost,
lure him here with my cries;
for these tear-stained blotches of thought
leave me empty inside.

I am left in the aftermath of your passing...
mourning the assassin's kill;
soul sliced opened to bleed me blind.
Chained and bound, I evade flirtatious eyes
to inhibit forbidden thoughts;
for love fled upon your precious wings,
survived only by silent memories.
I stand alone in the midst of this nightmare,
searching for you amongst a midnight dream.

The shawl of darkness enfolds me,
yet the stars elude my eyes
as the moon reigned misery;
night filled with sounds that hurt,
no peace to be found.
Silently, I stood waiting for dawn to set me free.
In the midst of the new day's calm and the sun's glory,
I saw you in the flight-path of the clouds,
arms outstretched,
calling my name through the zephyr's scream...
"love, come to me..."
Just mere steps into the convalescent sea.

Moments like This

The stars quickly dim,
taking their place behind stretching clouds
as the allure of night fades to light.
Morning's scent steals grace from sleep's convalescent ether...
rousing hearts and minds from delusional dreams
to don their disguise of a million lies...
reassembling to suffer daily.

And each tick of the clock mimics the hum
of my pulse... head in hands...
holding on to my makeshift sanity;
withholding eyes too jaded to see.
My frayed heart is wrapped in strands of tender,
one beat away from surrender;
anxiously timid, awaiting for yet another shoe to fall.
I keep to this intimate isolation...
for this world has proved incapable of trust.

But, oh, when the night comes and the blind moon rises...
taking its rightful place in the sky,
I lovingly stand within her sliver rain,
caught up in the frantic foreplay emanating from stars.
Inside the darkness, shadows span to fill
the emptiness and my consciousness,
giving way to blurry visions...
undressing these eyes with the presence of you.

And it's moments like this I have come to cherish.
This sensory state of existence,
exonerates me from misery's melody,
demanding its silence
in the inky hours of midnight's serenade.

Embraced

Lost; forever in this dysfunctional isolation without you.
I have crossed the void of a thousand Milky Ways,
slow danced in the arms of a crescent moon,
turned my back on all I have known,
replacing comfort for saline tears.
Hear my somber soliloquy;
forgive me for letting you down.

These faithful arms reach out to you,
as the precious scent of your ardor
awakens my sanity and the shroud that consumed me fades;
I am reborn again within the soft of your eyes.
Last night, the stars were shining... silken petals unfurled
as you slipped into me... wholly.

Precious Memories

Today is yet another day... spun inside out.
I am overstretched beyond my flesh... left empty once again.
Each day in life's ballets, more plagued than the last;
and even though tomorrow is only a schizophrenic dream,
I'll cherish its dawning... with mind bent and humbled.
There was a time when I embraced myself wholly...
a shining star among millions.
But a serpent's kiss and obscene hands sent me falling
like a pebble tossed into a turbulent sea;
caught up in its waxing and waning tide
without purpose or destination,
never leaving tiny ripples to skip count... 1... 2... 3.
Now I sit waist-deep, masturbating in self-pity,
seduced by insecurity... deaf and numb
to words calling out from my lacerated heart.
I am infected with fears fearing fears... nearly drowning,
yet thankful for these eyes sewn shut...
sealing in those precious memories.

Time's Ceasing

Come to me in the silence of the night,
before the hall clock chimes of time's passing.
Let your footsteps fall like an urgent pulse,
vying for life, where the soul is understood.
'Neath the knotty arms of the old Oak tree,
I will wait for you in Midnight's shadow.
Come to me in the silence of the night;
gather me in the warmth of your embrace.
Free the words that lay restless on my tongue;
your mouth on my mouth is the soul of me.
Come, let us part sweetly before the dawn,
for tomorrow's light is not ours to share.

Oft in the distance, a mockingbird cries
one last time; one last time before it dies.

Forget Me Not

I stood in the midst of the meadow,
as Autumn's breeze swayed its flaxen hair.
The last flush of sun was giving way
to a peach-blossoming sky,
readying the day to lay and replenish
beneath the lull of night.

As it unfolded around me,
I watched with daydream eyes
as visions of you etched upon a lowering cloud
slipped by in outstretched shadows...
just out of reach of my trembling hand;
for dreams still held you captive within its grasp.
I held myself with tired arms, weighted with sadness
as my heart grew threadbare thin;
another tear-stained page stored in memory...
those painful forget-me-nots.

Until

Pearl of my heart, we must journey home,
bid farewell to yesterday's dead sun.
For storm clouds have gathered to slice the moon;
we must go before these arid sands of misfit time
cease to flow.

And we cannot add another hour,
for seconds break not only the day,
but steals the ease of my spirit...
and I have no more gooselike tears to feed the jester;
because this is so, love... we must part.

Walk close; let our footsteps fall as one,
leaving primrose-stained impressions,
as a legacy of our passing,
like un-framed wisps of art.

Come, we'll trace the moon back to the stars,
where abandoned hearts, never to be forgotten,
breathe the breath of the Beloved.
There, we'll rest and lay sweetly until longing rises
and we beckon to be love's slave again.

Alas, we'll return one day, at another time,
another space beneath a blue moon's dawning;
come let us go, never to look back with eyes of regret;
remember, Pearl of my Heart,
there's no need to say good-bye.

A Small Lament

Please...
do not look away,
I am more than what you see.
I have no claims or expectations;

I am
more than innocence fleeing;
more than flesh and blood.
I have a soul as well.

I am
one of life's precious reminders,
its fruit on the fringe of fullness...
even though my skin is scarred
and dirty beneath
this frayed and tag-rag dress.

I am
the essence of this land and place...
yet placeless;
the mirrored gaze
of countless faces...
neither brown
nor white.

I am
imagination,
that will never be
imagined.

Can
you say some words to me,
born from your heart,
that your lips can proclaim?

Today,
I left a message for you,
inscribed within my eyes
and the draw of my smile;
even though embosomed by despair.
You see...
mere seconds of life
are celebrations,
no time to waste
on bootless tears.

Oh,
how I long for the day
when we will transcend
these mortal constraints.
Until then, I am alone,
a traceless gem...
patiently waiting
for you to turn
and see me.

Eyes

Her delicate
silhouette still lingers,
closer than these arms can embrace;
haunting me.
I breathe her in...
within the lull of a zephyr;
lilac and roses
fill the air...
staining my memory.
Life
found her defenceless,
silenced by a veil of fear.
Faith
was clutched tight within her hands,
as esoteric dreams
laid shattered beneath
rages of a strange
and soulless
hand.

Frail
she emerged... soul hidden,
draped in shades of deathly grey.
Sweet serenity
severed tragically;
incarcerated
reality.

Her
taunting whispers bleed my heart,
no peace for the buried hurt inside;
for innocence was laid to rest
long before dying.

She's
no longer earthbound,
yet, I smell... I feel...
tiny caresses...
intimately weaving in...
and out, through me.

I
no longer find release
in the sting of these saline tears,
and the shrouds of nightmares live on
through the light of day.

She
wore candy apple red
the day she left;
oh, how her bright eyes smiled.

Unspoken

Leather-bound dreams, trapped on parchment pages,
fading to dust on each new day's gloaming;
this villa and pell-mell heart's my cage.
I peer through transition lattices; blind,
no conscious thought that your heart was roaming.
Passion spilled in abundance, you maligned.

Loves ambrosial tears, now crumbs of rages,
bleeding memories on the white of heart;
your tainted lips will haunt me for ages.
So much for wanting you; tainted ink stain.
Stoic, I'll stitch the seams that came apart
and heal my wounded spirit from this pain.

Leather-bound dreams, trapped on parchment pages,
loves ambrosial tears, now crumbs of rages.

In the Arms of an Angel

Last night, I lay in the arms of an angel,
within the swerve of his limbs and hips
as the ebon suede of night unfolded.
Nothing was as it appeared to be;
no longer earthbound anymore.
We rose and fell across a jealous sky,
drifting past the salient eyes of moon and stars,
where dreams soar to invade without boundaries.

He serenaded me with beguiling love songs,
easing the pulse of my heart
while the sweet of his breath aroused my flesh...
rekindling the beauty of my soul's refrain.
I lay like less than an angel
as he parted the curtain of my being.
Soft he gazed upon my wants and needs,
cradling the ache of my enslaved hunger.

And the cadence of the night made no sound;
caught up in the gasp of its own trembling.
He ensnared all tragic memories
and gifted me with epitaphs of pleasure.
And poetry flowed with spellbound imagery,
delicate lines of lyrical seduction.
Hence, his words aroused the swirling air,
vowing his love... mine to forever keep.

Last night, I lay in the arms of an angel,
feeding desires now doused in flames;
all that I longed for, fed by his intimate possession.
Now today, I miss the kiss he smeared upon my lips,
and the words he used... to make love to my soul.

Vertigo

Round and round in this dance of life.
Is there no solace within the noise?
These celestial seducers have let me down...
left to tender a mind inanely caught up
in a love that bleeds me insane.

Up and down on metaphor's sheets,
making love to words that's wooed me all day;
a mere sex-frayed cliché in a filthy tabloid,
barren of quotes, verse and rhyme.

Round and round, up and down,
in faithless dreams I linger;
a spiritless ballerina with amputated legs,
daring to dance beneath a tragic moon.

If I could find lyrical eyes in this vertigo,
I'd hush and detain these impressions of me.
But, alas, I'm drunk on a swig of domestic-blotched ink;
now, come... watch me spill and soak the ground.

Confessions

In the quiet reverence of this moment,
sorrow wears tragic upon my face,
for all that we wanted yesterday and today
still dangles on the fringes of a maybe...
someday, dawning.
And with each failed footstep,
patience wears thin,
eroding the pathway to our nirvana.
Yet love would not free
us its embrace;
we are drawn like bees
to the sweetness of its lily,
eager to inhale the fragrance
of its redolent breath.
I feel you, hear you,
spill you in my poetry;
and though this ache tears at my seams,
its bleeding is intoxicating,
I'd gladly suffer the wound
to keep my sanity.

I embrace you in the forever of my heart,
etched upon my soul,
your name stained upon my lips,
labeled as yours, eternally;
For though our love eluded this earthly realm,
it has been written in scriptures
by the divine.
So, if not in this life,
then surely in the next;
I will be waiting,
for I am yours,
and you are mine.

Flight of Love

Vanished forever is my dream of love,
Its flight untimely... barren in trust,
Words, unmasked illusions
the heart just could not see.
It once took form
when the earth smelled sweet,
when soft kisses and tender caresses
made me quiver,
and my body wore the pearls
of your seed.
When I was once the sweet balm
to your spirit,
and you, the bridegroom
to my sex.

We were son and daughter
of celestial companions;
sun and moon rising.
But the night is gone,
and our day has
been set free.
We have left our stain upon a pale blue sky,
withered flowers littering our pathway,
and the footsteps we once brushed
upon stretches of sand,
have been washed away by saline
remnants of rain.
Vanished
forever is my dream of love,
kept nostalgic inside of me.
Embezzled by an uninspired muse
of a Nightingale...
who could not sing.

Sweet Release

I cast my eyes across the endless sea,
praying for your return,
cursing the tides that carried you away;
and what once was,
is now what used to be.
Constant thoughts of you
invade my mind,
dreading the empty days and nights
spent wishing upon deaf stars...
brings no peace
to this heart.
Perchance to dream,
I'll give way to sleep,
for in slumber pose
your presence creeps,
gifting me with sweet release.

Seasons Change

He came unannounced... in early springtime...
just as the snowdrops... were stretching through the soil.
As I watched the delicate bulbs dance above ground...
my heart fluttered from breath to breath... sensing his presence.
The air around me... filled with the scent of him.
He aroused the tender of my skin... for his touch...
caressed with the sweet of blossoming fingers.
His steps fell silent... like the sun does to the ground...
yet my soul felt him moving about... opening doors and windows.
Washed with a healing breeze... I knew that this someone...
loved something in me... this truth brought tears to my eyes.
He invoked love from within... just as my ashes rose to life again.
He is faithful... always comes to find me... before my soul erodes.

The Birth of Passion

Sweat

I have traipsed across
the want of his skin...
seeking... that unmistakable
scent of his desire.

I have crouched beneath
the thunder of his pulse...
and prayed for rain...
to seep through the wall
of these urging needs...
silencing the beg of my flesh.

For I am immersed within
the wake of his fever...
captured by his kiss...
a captive of his hips...
And I demand a sip
from the fire that draws me in...
replenishing the thirst
between the fuel and I.

I crouched beneath
the thunder of his pulse...
hand in hand to dance with the flame.
Baptized with words filled with
rhythmic semantics...
an aged bottle of cognac...
lucid reflections...
the delicate outlines of
love under will... and sweat.

Stirring Echoes

Your echoes always reach me,
though they travel from afar,
o'er oceans and vast mountains,
no matter where you are.
Oh, how I long to linger
in their warm embrace,
lost in its sensual rapture,
while seeking visions of your face.
The memories of your loving
are etched on me inside,
and I still feel you moving,
still feel the passion in your ride.
Can you feel me reaching
to claim what I so miss,
the comfort of your body,
the hunger for your kiss?
I yearn again to taste you,
come return your love to me,
and calm this raging storm;
come feed this need in me.

Before Morning Comes

Tonight... dressed in Eve's translucent gown,
heart woven in intricate strands and delicate seams,
Innocence lies at my back... still swirling in my vigor...
and night, with its tranquil lullabies...
cannot hush my salacious thoughts...
nor ease the want in my restless flesh.

The illuminable rites began at dawn...
bewitched... possessed in the dance...
I ignited new flames... as the cautious sun peeks...
unveiling to reveal the unforgettable.

My will is detained in this moment,
disciplining the eagerness in my hunger,
here amid the misty fragrance of your essence...
and the lure of your taunting silhouette.
If I said, "Your love's my only company,"
would you turn and see my soul?
For without your eyes reflecting me...
I am just pretending to be... begging to be loved.

Soft fingers of the morning breeze soon will be stirring...
come, let us greet it with our thunder.
I will close my eyes... hold my breath
to fall as rain upon your famished land.
Say yes to the radiance in my eyes...
bask in the throe of this given moment...
and I'll seep through you... enthrall your dreams
until you come with me... or take me.

When Morning Comes

Morning finds me still wrapped in Eve's translucent gown,
heart still woven in love's intricate strands and satisfied seams,
still doused with the feral scent of his flesh,
still drunk on the love and hunger in his breath.
Now sweet innocence lies famished at my back,
lost inside the aria of passion's reverb.

Countless times... we made love
through restless days... endless nights,
drenched with the sweat of our eagerness.
And dew's wet tongue clung to skin
like sheer lingerie... urging pursuit of the prize.
His sleight of hand... a fix to the flesh...
erupting the coveted treasure.

And when morning comes... it finds me....
still breathless... lips still sealed within his kiss,
still addicted and detained within his heat,
still braced within his smile and misty stare,
still beguiled by his shine... the familiar in his eyes

Interlude

The light wraps me tender... in its shimmer
as his mouth seeks the purpose of my essence...
and I lay drunk from his arousing words and long kisses...
in this moist climate... this happy hour of the night.

He revealed my depth... swallowed my thirst... hunger...
space... and time... the Oh's and Ah's of my flesh
till I'd dare not speak of my pulse upon his altar...
for I am forever devoted to the ache in his greed.

Dawn... and I still recall the scent of him... seeds of love.
Alas... the moon and I are alone,
and the ripples from the wakes refuel my surge...
he loved me... fed me, and here I stand,
close to the edge... awaiting his return.

In Lieu of Sandcastles

My coming...
always a welcomed love of mine.
For a brief moment,
I thought it dead; yet, this morning,
when I awakened to the voice
of the undulating wind blowing in my ear,
it rose and came without warning...
leaving me to ponder the lascivious nature
of my thoughts and the unrequited dew
gathered fondly on my southern rose.
My, my, love's draft is
full bodied and
provocative
today.

Quietly, like the clouds flirting with the wind,
I strolled the nostalgic path along
the eastern horizon,
where a panting tempest still hovers
above our receding imprint.
I recall the day
when we danced bareback on white sand...
erasing the lines of purity
with timeless reverbs of passion;
today, I am not far from your touch.

Arise,
come meet me by the shore,
in the clearing by the rocks,
where we last made love.
Remembrance of that time leaves me hungry...
gather your fervent heat,
stoke the wild smell of your
delicious tears... so I may once again
quench my thirst.

Let us delight in the day,
engage in sights and sounds
as we touch... taste with lips and fingers.
Do you recall the salt-licked sonnet
you scribed along my spine?
There was no scenery more telling than this;
torn gown and panties round my feet...
sand in my hair... clinging to back and hips.

They say that a maiden wears
linen shoes as white as the Madonna lily.
Alas, desire has claimed my heart,
seduced this flesh....
now wearing the redolent scent of yours.
I was designed to be a barefoot woman.
I love the cool wet of earth between my toes;
it is fortunate... for these linen shoes
never did fit.

Choice

The year's in limbo... made a skeptic of me,
but by night... passion cultivates
the seeds nursed by the reveries
from the cradle of darkness.
Love sprouts in folds... and you...
hum my name through the night...
until a new dawn arrives once more.

Love is no stranger today...
Love parts the clouds...
Love renews a heart once torn and soiled...
now rekindled in a gown of desire.
The sun in my life rides
bareback upon the wind...
the old me lays bleeding as love
peels away frenzied fears...
fault lines of regret;
my heart has let down her hair again...
and I am musing with anticipation.

I dared recycle the old nightmares
just to test the power of love again.
Nightly, I stood staring
at the moon and stars...
craving to see the beauty in them...
as all lovers do...but I stood
too far to feel the ache in your kiss,
too far to wipe the tears from your eyes...
Still too far to touch your Love...
So, I keep you here... safe in my heart.

Encased in this silence, I stand naked;
longing for the heat of your eyes to
trace a path upon my lonesome fate...
wrap my heart in your forgiving flesh...
forsaking grays for pastel colors.
The key to my heart lies unattended;
there are no rules of engagement...
just the want of your hand in mine.

Blinds drawn round in a circle,
Silhouette seized and hushed,
as night's ebon finger strokes
the purr of my pulse.
The choice has always been... only yours,
for my heart's devotion outdates my breath.
My choice was made long before
I would ever come to know your name...
long before my love became yours.

Here I Stand

A gentle bat of the eyes
weaves a spell that storms the heart;
a subtle caress rouses intimate thoughts...
resonating like syllables of spoken words
across the want of flesh.
And a kiss from lips tendered with passion
rushes through these veins with ornaments of lust.
Enslaved by this cradled ache and a love that yields,
the will surrenders and lay
to consummate its devotion.

Each day, I dissolve as rain,
tracing the source of my hunger,
and every night in conjured dreams
urgent yearnings in an orb of light
ease the crave of my thirst;
it is then that I recall the quivering breaths of yesterday.

Now, as the morning haze
with hues like translucent ink,
paints the lay of the day
like a page torn from memory...
I sit and write these words, no less grateful,
for... today, like countless days before...
I thought of you again...
and these moments seize and erect my attention,
remembering... this heart has been taken for ransom.

Oh, how I cherish this love that has come to consume me;
and this I know to be true...
nothing else moves me...
just the lull of a Southern breeze and you.

Supplication

Be still, my love, let me breathe you in;
my breath flowers like the stars.
Let these eyes with wild lashes
decrease this space between us.
Bar the door and come to me,
for the sun has set...
and the flame has been tendered.

My palms braced upon your shoulders,
lean your back against the want of flesh;
I'm a yearning woman in earthly undress,
and the moonlight wraps my flesh.
Moisture is clinging to secret places,
and I am postured for the state of surrender.
Draw the curtains, love,
for the night has a million eyes.

The Muse Comes Out at Night

When night comes,
my intoxicated soul rises out of time,
shedding the sweating walls of the past
to glide upon mockingbird's wings
through locked doors and boarded windows,
to dance reeling and twitching,
wrapped within temptation's shawl
of orchids and roses... seducing dreams.

Never late, yet never early,
the blind moon enfolds about me
with the soft of its shine,
igniting bewitched words to escape my lips,
words born from such and such hunger.
So tired of enduring the disdain of dry humps
from impotent devotion,
that deludes my thoughts.
Embezzled platitudes fail to seize the madness
and prejudice
of life's one-sided compromises.

A brush by the breeze infiltrates my armour,
and I'm doused with back to back thrusts
while yearning hips and precocious lips
ooze with sweet nectar from bareback mounts
at the carnal juncture.
The hush of night only heightens the relentless,
rhythmic beat from climax's familiar echo,
a sound that breaks the barrier and soars
across the heat of my flesh... again...
and again;
so reminiscent of the coveted quivers of my glory days.

Tendered words swirl about,
painting murals of passion across the sky.
They were so decadent and inviting that I
engaged my shadow to catch the red eye to the stars
and harness the glowing radiance of their surge;
so drawn in to their flame that binds the thrill of love.
The air was rabid with ecstasy,
cornering and enticing me with the thirst for tender kisses,
while love's lucidity grazed itself over me...
summoning desire and lusty attention of the prize.

Midnight's elusive magic is shrouded
by the unbridled spell of the mind's imagination.
It is siphoned through the hunger of a full moon
and the bold scent of sex.
Alas, I am only a voyeur here,
anxious to gasp and dissolve
into a luscious pulse of sheer pleasure
before the prison walls and windows call my soul back
to its medicated body and its emotional scars.
Inside the space of time,
I'm but an overused toss within a faceless game...
found wanting and seldom understood.

Carnal Memories

The bed beneath us laid spread eagle,
aroused and anxiously enthused to
swallow our hunger;
storing memories as echoes
in the creaking bedsprings.

Our bodies knew no bounds
as we slid down...
between sweating bedsheets.

One light from a perfumed lamp
gathered us within its shadow...
boosting the yearning of the prize
as we succumbed to first contact;
captive hips... perched thighs.

Your hands teased. Kisses wide...
wet; fingers in my mouth sucking
where your essence still lingers.
You dipped as I dripped
around you...
begging for consumption.

All clarity of thought lost
as your tongue spoke wildly inside seams;
hair hugging my fingers.
Sighs turned to whimpers when
I unleashed in squirts;
your tongue pierced
and uncorked the wine,
stringing pearls upon Valhalla...
your home between my thighs.

Now the gossiping walls
are sweating while reminiscing;
the air hangs heavy
with the scent of pure sex,
and the moon is blushing
with naked shame,
slowly stroking herself
with well-placed fingers.

Thigh Chi

The fragrant lips of love's precious Lily
awakens the eyes of her beloved
without words or touch.
Her beauty unfolds its smoothed sheath...
unveiling the pearl;
as palpable as pulse against one's finger.
The scent of her nectar arouses the air;
her bloom... always in season.
Come, south wind, blow softly
like a breeze that caresses the skin.
For the Lily's bloom is but an awakened passion
rooted inside the beauty of one's secret garden

A Lover's Passion

I awakened, intoxicated with love,
spinning and whirling
in its light and sultry shadow.
I laid parched and watching
as love's touch formed me
like putty in ecstasy's heat.
I am drunk on its scent
in this private vertigo;
once a forgotten melody,
emerged within your precious song.

Wrapped in silk, tied with tremors...
All can see my heart's pulsing.
In this haze of love's quivering kiss,
I confess... my heart has been stolen.
In this fog, I have lost my way,
yet this love enfolds me;
this is home.
I have opened the gate for love,
for I long to wade in its streams of passion.

Beneath the sanctum
of love's streaming hunger,
his flesh provokes delicate tears
nestled inside my sin...
tender he whispers,
"forever in you."

Songbirds serenade the breeze,
and a million smiles erode the sky,
for love's pale halo is perched
high upon these breasts,
and I am enslaved beneath its spell.
I have lost my senses...
beckoning love's flame.

I am drunk on a sip,
a fire yet to come...
You have consumed my fate,
I have stepped out of myself
to drink from your wine,
and the aftertaste lasts forever.

After Glow

The smell of lust and sex still lingers in the air,
and I lay here in the midst of it all,
still reeling from aftershocks,
yet craving you inside.
Still reliving the eruptions that fired off eruptions;
the spiralling of your touch,
the feel of your hair in my hands,
the cadence of your thrust.
My belly tightens as it did
when dancing to your sway,
my legs still bear the imprints
of your shoulders,
where I braced and embraced.

My breast are still marked
by the pearls I wore,
where they hung and slapped
repeatedly to untamed rhythms
encased within our ecstasy.

My buttock is still aroused
From the heat of your breath,
sex lips swollen, quivering
from laps of tongue
tattooing the stretch of your crest.

My knees burn from where
I crawled to claim your prize,
the evidence of our releasing
lingers on...
in-between my thighs.

Damn these thoughts have me quivering,
all the way deep into my soul;
still caught up in
the afterglow.

Taunts

Let me talk to her,
the Dark One whispers
in my desire-stroked ears.
Let me hear what I
have yet to touch.
Let me consummate
in my mind
what my body craves
to consume.
Let me hear those lips
housed between
milky thighs.
Let me hear those quivers
released just before
she drools from those
succulent
sighs.
Put her on,
let me hear...
he whispers,
don't deny
me tonight.

Bemoaning Cadence

Last night I made love to loneliness,
surrendered to its embrace.
Unable to be lulled by my breathing...
heart beating;
caught up in the seduction of my frailties.
My hand not yours seeking to release me
as I lay here in the dark.
I summoned your memory,
became a voyeur to scenes of you
and I against the wall,
yet failing to ease myself;
for you see, the heart...
could not fool the mind,
and the hand could not brace
the ache within my prize...
It's so cold here without you.
Last night, I laid in pieces,
waiting for the dawn to come free me.
To pardon me of my sin...
suppress what's in my heart.
I am enslaved... possessed
by what is and what could be.

You tattooed your love on my heart,
left me with evidence of hunger
on these soiled fingers...
pleading oozing from my lips.
This is merely love bites....
I want bare back ridings...
below... beneath...!
I'm so close to the edge...
and these hands keep reaching in and out...
wrenched with desire.

Loveless Heat

Breathless...
eager to feel the quiver of her pulse
in the marrow of his bones.
Eager for him to lay claim
and emblaze her with his kiss,
unleashing all that remains
of her virginal secrets.

Anticipation
dances across the twitch of her salacious tongue,
leaving meaningless words tripping on syllables;
her thoughts of being licked and seduced
spirals the surge of moment
that oozes with dulcet sighs.

Her fervent skin,
wet like the calescent rains of August,
clinging to the heaving rhythm of each curve,
grazing the pulse of her sex.
The fuse was lit.

Her knees tremble
as she lay silent,
oozing from her pouty lips...
now roused by this nightly instigating dream.
She's a slave to the fierceness in her conjured muse.

Yet,
he feels so close tonight,
somewhere between her rabid need
and his salacious fix.
But alas, she's shaken and awakened
from the instigating shadows of her dream.
Once more she's left with only empty in her real;
left with her lonely lover's hand, just fingertips away
from climbing the walls of her loveless heat.

Evocative

Naked, she laid covered
in the perfume of their liquid rapture,
hips and limbs aching,
shaking where he had cherished her
wild and sweet;
still brandishing the sheen from his intoxicated lust.
And she dared not move
from love's built fervent fire,
forever wanting to lay within the flame,
inhaling the sated air
of their essence
while clutching
gifted pearls;
reminiscing.

Insomnia

How can I sleep; how can I sleep
when lusty thoughts are rampant and aroused,
awakening the sweet place of my ambrosial tears.
My suffering breasts are at high noon
on this empty night that's dying;
please, do not let the moon draw its curtain
before we come together again.

My love,
I am in need of breathless kisses,
amorous lips and knowing hands
to ease the heave of my pulse
at the carnal juncture.
Only you can release this rain.

How can I sleep; how can I sleep
when I am here and you are there;
my life is but a cycle of deaths
each morning to morning.
You promised me your heart,
now come within my reach.

I lay awake
with a sigh on the edge of my lips,
a dare within my kiss
and a beggar's gaze,
hungry...
wild with demands.
I am drunk
on what could be;
each day finds me arrested inside,
nostalgia on recall
and your words circling my flames...
Tell me, how can I sleep?

Without You

In dreams I wander through the instigating shadows,
hoping to catch just a glimpse of your face.
Alas, the darkness has no eyes,
and all I can sense is the brief touch of your hand.
I try to speak, but the words spill
and stain my lips with tears...
leaving only the beat of my heart
and the heat of my breath to say,
I miss you;
miss your precious smile,
the light inside your eyes,
miss your whispers in my ear
as your fingers gently stroke my hair,
miss the hunger in your kiss,
the cadence of your hips,
and those eruptions that filled
me with aftershocks
that lingered on for days.
How cruel the night is
to leave me blind,
teasing me with token dreams
that condemn me half,
not whole,
here without you.

Moonlight Seduction

Last night, the sultry moon came,
dropped her diaphanous gown like an overzealous Jezebel,
wanderlust, impatient to lie above and beneath me,
eavesdropping on the hum of my pulse.
With an earnest attempt at the prize,
her savvy fingers splayed the knot of my undress;
I met her with closed eyes as lust slow-danced upon my skin.

She came spilling instigating verbs full of anticipation,
lighting fires within my verve... in candlelight's swoon.
She was fluid in motion, robust as wine with hunger in her eyes,
enslaving me within her sexual vigour.
Morning stole provocation from her embrace
when she rose as the sun flexed his arms,
laying claim to her shine.
Still, this ache is braced beneath the touch of my hand;
I'm but a junkie in need of a fix.

More Than

I want to be more
than your lover...
I want to be the one you turn to
when all else in the world holds no succour
and your soul seeks refuge.
I want to be the forever in your heart
Once-wrecked by goodbyes.

I want to be your next breath
that's just a soul-kiss away,
the heartbeat that keeps you
from crossing over into heaven's gate,
those stirring thoughts in your mind
set on instant replay.

I want to be the hand that reaches down
to stroke you when your body
is hungry with needs.
I want to be the look born from your face
when you release alone
what you release in me.

I want to be your river
of dreams and fantasies,
to fulfil those things left untouched
and empty by others.
I want to be the one
who gives your life meaning.
I want to be more
than just your lover.

Awakening

It was midnight, beneath a blue moon's dawning,
when I first walked into the center of your heart
and made love to your soul.
Oh, my love, I have loved you for many lifetimes.
Once again, fate has seized us and love is renewed.

I remember the shine in your limpid eyes that held me spellbound,
as they do at this moment, and as they forever shall be.
Your scent has coursed through my veins since last we touched;
it has awakened me... now my walls and I are sweating with anticipation.

If only I could part the sky like the linen curtains in my room.
I'd bring you close, so close... that I may become
the flame that fuels your muse, the ecstasy in your pen,
the gasps from your parted lips...
when I become the hand upon your thigh.
I'd be inclined to kiss your insatiable lips, brace the need...
the ache between and once again consummate our love.
For we are destined to spend endless days... endless fervent nights
fulfilling our fated prophecy; there will always be a you and I...
past blue skies... to the moon and back; I love you

Dream a Little Dream

Naked, I laid beneath a blanket of stars,
seduced by grace and a teary-eyed moon's quiver.
Its silhouette danced upon the want of my flesh
and lingered like the heat of a lover's touch.
Each caress of its gaze... like slow sips of vintage wine...
toppling my inhibitions to rise like Midnight's tide.

I miss you, my love; for tonight the ruptured sky is silent
and the ink of my soul is smeared and intoxicated...
I lay here revisiting your words, and...
today... I missed the hunger of your kiss.
I'm held prisoner inside this abyss...
so I dared conjure a concubine muse
to disarm my flesh... to dream a little dream of you.
The beauty I felt sustained and held my breath,
staining a kiss upon these lips... for a lifetime to remember;
the air itself was christened with the scent of you.
And even though the ache of my heart lay scattered,
the want of my flesh has been fasting far too long...
"Please come, love... I'm empty, fill me...
leave me drunk and stumbling."

I laid naked beneath the stars,
and as the pulse of time was moved to hush...
then suddenly, there you were... watching me.
A million stars appeared, whispering your name;
we spoke through eyes...
what lips could never convey.
Tonight, you laid with me in my dreams.
How I envy the night and dreams
where we play... hide and seek.

Southern Nights

In the still of the night, beneath a blue moon's rising,
shadows scattered from east to west,
and the southern wind quickly stepped aside
as the heat of my lover's breath...
gathers around the mocking limits of my flesh.
He seeped between the stitches of my seams...
to peel away the fabric of my disguise...
freeing the mind... laying with my heart
to unchain the shackles from my soul.
Eager to consume his love,
I savored the fever in his kiss
as I recalled the sinful aroma of his passion;
some memories never fade away.
He stormed my dreams to reign over them...
aroused me with his lingering caresses.
His eyes forever watching me from within...
unencumbered by sedated memories,
misplaced walls and trails of tears.

He baptized me with words...
parted the waters to plunder my sea...
he doused me with his warmth throughout my bones...
giving me something to fight for again today.
And with each pulse of my heart,
he moved in and out through me...
Now here I sit, drenched in desire...
alas, too far to embrace this ache in my imagination...
Love is Fierce.

The Constant Gardener

Frenzied dreams with its sleight of hand,
has once again... lured me here,
to the insatiable beg
of the constant gardener.
Where wild songs are being played
on fine-tuned strings of marmalade
and jasmine; alas, tongue tied
lyrical fornications...
will never have words.

Beguiled by the unholy melody,
I hushed the lips of my lascivious temptress;
held her suspended in thoughts of satisfaction...
for devious are her moans.

The moon is dressed in desire tonight,
and the erogenous glow
of a thousand stars are poised...
and distracted, by the tick-tock sway
of my fevered hips.

I peered through eyes of subtle glances...
yet, I stood too close... finding
an ever-enthused garden...
climbing the beat of a sinful pulse.

The intoxicated pussy willows
were drenched between the thighs of purple passion...
as the drooping ball shrubs stood like phallic symbols...
easing from the lips of a Lily in bloom.

It was more than a mind could gather,
more than mere sight could interpret.
Yet, I stood spellbound within the moment...
sweating like rain on sheer lingerie.

Oh, passion, sweet seducer
who transcends more than the pulse of this rose
between my fingers... who beckons
flesh to your bidding... I cry mercy;
your tempest soars tonight
between the gasps.
These mellifluous tones
are rabid and ensnared...
by the rouge lips of the constant gardener...
who dared stepped out into the night.

And none can sleep
when the gardener's taking care;
for he's drunk on venom from an erect tongue...
and no man can sleep.

Spilling

He sauntered into the sweet spot
of my imagery...
slid inside the cadence
of its undulating flow,
laid twitching as I cajoled
him for hours,
lulled by titillating snares
of metaphors,
seduced
by
words.

He engaged in foreplay with my muse,
till dawn came with its rhythmic knocking;
flagrant inspiration
within the palm of my hand.

I scribed him with
the ink of my essence,
aroused him with
my sex scriptures.

He became the focus
of my soliloquy,
the roll of vowels,
kneading on a greedy tongue....
as these lips intercourse
down the pulsing vein
of adjectives and verbs,
lubricating him to fruition;
he is
my poetry.

One Hour

One hour with you
when the room is dappled with gold and red,
when wishes are flung away,
and desire flows wild... sweet;
there will be your palms on my shoulders,
your precious breath against my face;
provoked and submissive,
I will bare my all to you.

One hour with you
when I shower you with dreams long forgotten
and walk the hallways of your heart and mind
to shelter myself in the love you keep;
for one hour, I will no longer be homeless...
without you.

One hour tonight,
when I dare be bold to claim the surge
of your fevered vein within my hands
and tender your need with tongue-tracing kisses...
awakening your urge to morning wood.
For, tonight, I will unchain your soul,
stroke the source of your inspiration
within the swerve of my hips; lubricity of tongue...
until we lay suspended in the apex of satisfaction.

Just one hour with you
when you teach me to forget
the horrors of this world,
tragedies of the day;
and my soul slips into you
somewhere between
a whisper and a sigh.

Pieces of You and Me

Pieces of you dance behind these closed eyes,
intoxicating the surge of my senses;
my heart pulses like waves of a tempestuous ocean.
You have merged with me,
kissed and embraced me with tenderness.
And this is true, my love;
I am a beguiled drunkard...
in love with the splendour of you.
Slowly, I inhale and exhale,
for you are the fragrance of my breath...
catalyst of all that I desire,
igniting fires of pure passion...
dousing the well of my hunger;
your blood... my blood.

Pieces of you dance... born again within my chest;
through sun and rain, light and dark,
through sedated nights and disarming days.
And this is true, my love;
your smile is the essence of my greed,
shamelessly the arousal of my ardent addiction.
Your words smeared on my lips is a spell cast
upon the boldness of my ink;
endless hours with thoughts erect...
spilling poetry of you.

Pieces of you, like the trail of your hand across my skin,
rouses me like a rambunctious minx,
flushed with anticipation.
And the heat of your whisper in my ear provokes me to surrender.
Your every movement...
archived as cherished moments.
And this is true, my love;
the light in your eyes
orchestrates the rhythm of my dreams and reality.
At night, you come and lay over me
as the moon and stars cast intimate silhouettes
across the soul of our flesh.
And this is true, my love;
all that I am... is all of you;
Love is... pieces of you and me.

About The Author

   Tina began writing poetry, as well as short stories, at the age of eleven. Even at this early age, she used poetry to express those things in her heart that she could not articulate with spoken words. Poetry is the medium that she finds not only comfort and strength, but also an unleashing of joy, pain, healing and passion. Through her writings, she hopes to convey the many faces of love; how the heart and soul responds to the seesaw motions of love.

   Tina is a Registered Nurse who is currently completing her Bachelor's degree in both Psychology and Religion at Liberty University in Lynchburg, Virginia.

Acknowledgements

I want to first, give thanks to God for the many gifts and blessings that he bestows upon me each day. I also want to thank the following people for believing in me, for giving me unconditional love and encouragement to fulfill my endeavors.

To Nick, who left us too soon, who loved me through the good and the bad... never faltering in his belief in me.

To Brian and Kim... you inspire me to reach higher.

Last but certainly not least, to Moe Anthony who found me when I dropped my dream by the roadside, for pushing me to believe in myself again. Through his tireless effort, this book has become a reality!

I love all of you... to the moon and back!